What Is
the
Trinity?

Ralph O. Muncaster

HARVEST HOUSE PUBLISHERS
Eugene, Oregon 97402

Cover by Terry Dugan Design, Minneapolis, Minnesota

By Ralph O. Muncaster

Are There Hidden Codes in the Bible?
Can Archaeology Prove the New Testament?
Can Archaeology Prove the Old Testament?
Can We Know for Certain We Are Going to Heaven?
Can You Trust the Bible?
Creation vs. Evolution
Creation vs. Evolution Video
Does the Bible Predict the Future?
How to Talk About Jesus with the Skeptics in Your Life
How Do We Know Jesus Is God?
Is the Bible Really a Message from God?
Science—Was the Bible Ahead of Its Time?
What Is the Proof for the Resurrection?
What Is the Trinity?
How Is Jesus Different from Other Religious Leaders?
What Really Happened Christmas Morning?
What Really Happens When You Die?
Why Does God Allow Suffering?

WHAT IS THE TRINITY?
Examine the Evidence Series

Copyright © 2001 by Ralph O. Muncaster
Published by Harvest House Publishers
Eugene, Oregon 97402

Library of Congress Cataloging-in-Publication Data

Muncaster, Ralph O.
    What is the Trinity? / Ralph O. Muncaster.
        p. cm. — (Examine the evidence series)
    Includes bibliographical references.
    ISBN 0-7369-0613-4
        1. Trinity. I. Title

BT111.3 .M86 2001
231'.044—dc21   00-054185

Printed in the United States of America.

01 02 03 04 05 06 07 08 09 10 / BP / 10 9 8 7 6 5 4 3 2 1

Contents

Why Does the Trinity Matter?

Christians speak of the Holy Trinity, the three "persons" of God, as a foundational aspect of their faith. The Holy Trinity is the Father, the Son (Jesus), and the Holy Spirit—somehow existing as a single "God." At the very least it sounds confusing. Some people think it's irrational.

Why is the Trinity such an issue? Perhaps because it's basic to knowing God. After all, to know God, we should know *who He is* and *what He is like.*

The entire *Examine the Evidence* series attempts to point out the enormous importance of choosing a faith that is the truth. We all have a choice, and a wrong choice could be disastrous—for our life on earth and for eternity. Christianity gives us ample evidence to evaluate the truth. It stands or falls based on the truth of the Bible, which records the *historical facts* of God's dealings with human beings, unlike the thinly supported philosophies of other religions.

The Trinity is a biblical concept, carried throughout the Scripture.

> 1. The Bible defines God as three "persons."
>
> 2. We can trust the Bible's definition.

We will examine the evidence for trusting the Bible, then look at what the Bible says about God. Without an understanding of the real nature of God, we are merely praying to and worshiping some "thing" or, worse yet, a creation of our own imagination. *The Trinity is real and personal.*

The fact is, if we worship, pray to, and think we know a "god" who is not real, we are deceived. It is important to know the nature of the God we presume to know. The Trinity is the biblical and Christian definition. While it may be difficult to understand, if it is indeed a true description of God, we need to know enough to at least accept it. This book will attempt to clarify the issue of the Trinity so we can know who God is.

The Key Issues

1.
Is There an Authority That Speaks About the Trinity?
(pages 6–21)

2.
How Can Three "Persons" Be One God?
(pages 10–13, 24, 25)

3.
What Support Is There for the Trinity?
(pages 14–21, 24–39)

4.
Why Is the Trinity So Important?
(pages 40–44)

5.
What Do We Do As a Result?
(pages 45–47)

Why Consider the Bible an Authority?

There is vast evidence, including statistical proof, that an all-knowing God inspired the Bible. Here is a short summary with some examples.

1. The Bible's Prophecies[1]

One-hundred-percent accurate historical prophecy provides irrefutable "proof" that a God from beyond time and space inspired the Bible. Why? Because there are well over 600 historical (thus verifiable) prophecies contained in the Bible—with none ever shown to be wrong.

The odds of this happening without the involvement of God are inconceivable—considered "absurd" by statisticians. For example, just 48 of the prophecies about Jesus coming true in any one person by coincidence is like winning 22 state lotteries in a row with the purchase of one ticket for each. Put another way, the odds are similar to those of one person being struck by lightning 31 times.

Since these prophecies were written hundreds of years before Jesus' birth (which has been confirmed by archaeology), we know they were not contrived after the events. The prophecies were extremely specific, giving names of people, places, timing, and specific descriptions of unusual events. No other purported holy book contains even a few miraculous prophecies, let alone the hundreds found in the Bible.

2. Scientific Insights[2]

Similar irrefutable evidence of the divine inspiration of the Bible is found in over 30 amazing scientific insights recorded in the Bible more than 2000 years before science discovered them. The biblical writings are accurate in their references to:

- *Physics*—the first and second laws of thermodynamics, and more

- *Engineering*—the ideal dimensions of the ark for its purpose

- *Geology*—the hydrologic cycle, ocean currents, atmospheric phenomena, and more

- *Astronomy*—the earth is suspended in space, the earth is round, the difference between stars, and more

- *Medicine*—quarantine, sanitation, handling of the dead, and more

The Bible was not intended to be a science text, but a guide to human relationships with God. Even so, its references to science are all correct—though recorded centuries in advance of our time.

The Accuracy of the Creation Account

Scientists who thoroughly analyze the ten steps of creation described in Genesis 1 find that the order in which the steps are listed agrees with the order discovered by science.[2]

Point 1—When Moses recorded the events of creation in about 1500 B.C., no culture had any scientific knowledge about the universe, the conditions of the earth, or the animals, or how any of them were formed.

Point 2—At the time of Moses, no culture knew the *order* of the events of creation. The odds of just guessing the order correctly (even if the steps were known) is about one chance in four million—similar to the odds of winning a state lottery.

Was Moses just extremely lucky at guessing both the steps and the order? Or was he inspired by God?

3. Reliability of Biblical Manuscripts[3]

The original Old Testament manuscripts were holy Scripture—that is, a written record of words inspired by God. So vital was the accuracy of Scripture that any person claiming to speak for God who said anything that didn't prove to be true was to be put to death (Deuteronomy 18:20). Scribes—those whose profession was to copy the Bible—were highly respected and had many years of rigorous training. Many time-consuming cross-checks were made to ensure the accuracy of their work.[3,5]

Furthermore, the people of Israel memorized vast sections of Scripture, even entire scrolls. So any mistakes that might appear were quickly corrected. The miraculous accuracy of the Old Testament Scriptures was confirmed in 1947, when scrolls of all the books of the Old Testament (except Esther) were found—untouched for nearly 2000 years. Some of these "Dead Sea Scrolls" date back to nearly 300 B.C. All are virtually identical to the most recent Old Testament Hebrew texts.

Likewise, the reliability of the New Testament is shown by the more than 24,000 manuscripts from the early centuries of the church that are still in existence today. Though many of these manuscripts were not copied by highly trained scribes, there is still little difference among the thousands of copies. Moreover, the age of the manuscripts demonstrates that the New Testament writings were in wide circulation during the time of the eyewitnesses to the events recorded in those writings.[4] These eyewitnesses would not have tolerated widespread proliferation of errors.

4. Historical Accuracy[5,6,7]

The historical accounts in the biblical record display both precision and accuracy. In the late 1800s, it was widely believed that the Bible was full of historical errors. But when the world's most renowned archaeologists began to investigate the Bible, expecting to prove it wrong, they instead found it accurate to

the small est detail. Now the Bible is regarded as a major historical source for archaeology in the Middle East. Using the Bible, archaeologists of many different religions have discovered entire cities and cultures whose existence had been long forgotten.

Especially important are archaeological finds that support the God-inspired prophecies of the Bible. The Dead Sea Scrolls (see previous page) are but one example. Early copies of the Septuagint (a translation of Scripture made from Hebrew to Greek in about 280 B.C.) and other early translations also confirm the prophetic texts.

One of the most amazing prophecy-confirming finds was the "Cyrus cylinder," which records King Cyrus of Persia's decree allowing the return of the Israelites from exile. This decree had been prophesied by Isaiah about 200 years earlier—long before Cyrus was born (Isaiah 44:28). And archaeological evidence that confirms other prophecies from both the Old and New Testaments is abundant.

Defining the Holy Trinity

Webster defines the Trinity in the simplest terms:

> "The union of three divine figures, the Father, Son,
> and Holy Ghost, in one Godhead."[8]

Accurate from a biblical standpoint? Yes. Understandable to most people? No. Misleading? Possibly. (More description is necessary, the word "ghost" has changed in meaning over the last few centuries and now gives the wrong impression, and there is no mention of the co-equal, personal nature of the Trinity.)

A much better and more complete definition of the Trinity is given by a well-known theological dictionary. It defines the Trinity as:

> "The term designating one God in three persons. Although not
> itself a biblical term,...[it is] a convenient designation for the
> one God self-revealed in Scripture as the one essence of the
> Godhead. We have to distinguish three "*persons*" who are
> neither three gods on the one side, nor three parts or modes of
> God on the other, but *coequally* and *coeternally* God."[9]

Why Isn't the Word "Trinity" in the Bible?

As the above definition states, although the word "Trinity" never appears in the Bible, the concept is "self-revealed" by God, as will be clear throughout this book. Biblical scholars merely gave the concept of the three-in-one God a name so it would be easy to refer to and discuss.

There are other concepts in the Bible that have been given a name that doesn't appear in the Bible. For instance, the omnipotence ("all-powerfulness") of God is very clear from the Scriptures (for example, in Job 38 and 39). No Christian would deny this doctrine—yet the word "omnipotence" is never used in the English Bible. For ease of reference, the concept of God's "all-powerfulness" was given the name "omnipotence." The same is true of the word "Trinity."

The Trinity Is Three *Persons*

A "person" is someone who can know you, can counsel and help you, can care about you, and might even sacrifice himself for you. So the suggestion that God is an "it," or that the Holy Spirit is an "it," is essentially saying that God is a "force" that doesn't 1) know, 2) care about, 3) help, or 4) sacrifice itself for human beings. The Bible repeatedly states that God knows each of us, that He lovingly cares about us, that He counsels and helps us, and that He even sacrificed Himself for us. Clearly, God is not an "it."

The persons of the Trinity (Father, Son, and Holy Spirit), while co-equal and co-eternal, do fulfill different roles (see pages 28–41).

Three Persons, One God

It is certainly hard to conceive of a single God who exists in three persons. But once we recognize that God exists in dimensions far beyond our limitations of time and space, we can begin to see why we don't understand His complexity. There are various analogies that can help us understand a "three-in-one" God (see pages 26, 27), but for the purpose of discussing the Trinity at this point, let's just define God as one—composed of three persons.

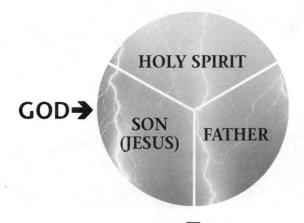

The Persons of Trinity Are Co-equal and Co-eternal

This description of the Trinity indicates that the Son and the Holy Spirit are totally equal with God the Father. At first glance, this seems to contradict the Bible. For instance, Jesus prayed to the Father in the garden of Gethsemane: "Not what I will, but what you will" (Mark 14:36). This seems to imply that the Father was above Jesus.

The answer is revealed by defining the *purpose* of Jesus while on earth. Jesus' purpose was to assume the role of humanity to become not only a sacrifice for human sin but also to teach us how to relate to an all-powerful, all-holy God. To accomplish this, Jesus "gave up" the right to exercise His power as God while He was on earth (this concept is called "kenosis" in theology). Jesus thus took on humanity with all its attributes. As a human, He taught us to pray to God. He taught us how to relate to God. And He taught us that the will of God is not always our will.

Did this short-term subjugation to God the Father make Jesus "less equal"? No! It served a teaching purpose. The Bible clearly describes Jesus as equal to God (for example, "I and the Father are one"—see John 10:30). Jesus also received worship and forgave sin, something only God could do. And Jesus proclaimed His ultimate authority as God: "All authority in heaven and on earth has been given to me" (Matthew 28:18).

The eternal existence of Jesus along with the Father is evident in John chapter 1. Jesus is a person of the Godhead from the beginning to the end (Revelation 22:13). Likewise, the Holy Spirit is a person of the Godhead who is co-equal and exists from beginning to end. Notice that in the *beginning* (Genesis 1:2) the Spirit of God hovered over the surface of the deep. Also, at the *end of time*, the Spirit of God is a gain present (Revelation 22:17).

The Trinity in the Old Testament

There is substantial evidence supporting the concept of the Trinity in the Old Testament (the Hebrew Scriptures). Apart from the individual references to each of the three "parts" of the Trinity, we also find other indications that God is made up of multiple "natures," or better, "persons." For example:

The very first reference to God in the Bible implies the Trinity.

Genesis 1:1 states, "In the beginning God created the heavens and the earth." The Hebrew word used here for God is *Elohiym*. This is very significant because the word *Elohiym* is plural (the "iym" at the end is like adding an "s" in English). In fact, e*lohiym* is frequently used in reference to multiple gods. However, the grammatical context in Genesis 1:1 and elsewhere clearly indicates a supreme *single* God.

Notice further that, when God is referred to at the creation of mankind (Genesis 1:26), the words are, "Let us make man in our image." Again, this refers to the plural nature of a single God, which is made clear by the grammar.

The first of the Ten Commandments (Exodus 20:2,3) gives us a clear picture, again, of the importance of the singular God in three persons context. It states, "I [singular] am the LORD your God [*Elohiym*, plural], who brought you out of Egypt, out of the house of slavery. You shall have no other gods [same word, *elohiym*, plural] before Me [singular]." Here again, God reveals Himself in language as a single God in essence, with multiple "persons" that comprise Him—thus, not three different gods, but *one*.

God the Father

God the Father is presented in the Old Testament in absolute, total glory. So holy and so glorious is His majesty that it was believed that anyone who saw His face would die (Genesis 32:30; Isaiah 6:1-5).

The presence of God the Father (*theophany*—see insert) was perceived in many miraculous ways:

- An angel appeared to Hagar (Genesis 16:9)
- The Lord appeared to Abraham (Genesis 18:1-15)
- The Lord appeared again to Abraham (Genesis 22:11,12)
- The burning bush to Moses (Exodus 3:2)
- Clouds and fire to the Israelites (Exodus 14:19)
- The tabernacle (Exodus 40:34)
- The Lord appeared to Moses (Exodus 33:11)
- The Lord appeared to Isaiah (Isaiah 6:1-5)
- A fourth "man" appeared in the fiery furnace with Shadrach, Meshach, and Abednego (Daniel 3:25)

What Is a *Theophany?*

A *theophany* is a visual or spoken presence of God. There were many theophanies in the Old Testament (such as the burning bush—see Exodus 3:2), possibly because God needed to provide unmistakable evidence of His divine authority over the rebellious nation of Israel.

Some theophanies clearly show the glory of God (for example, the presence of the Lord on Mount Sinai—Exodus 19:18,19; the cloud over the tabernacle—Exodus 40:34). Other theophanies are apparently manifestations of God in human form—often described as the appearance of "an angel of the Lord," a term which implies a special reverence reserved for God. Scholars debate many issues about "angel of the Lord" theophanies. Some believe they are appearances of Christ before He came to earth as a human being.

God the Son

The Old Testament is also filled with writings that point toward Jesus. There are hundreds of prophecies contained in the Old Testament that are exactly fulfilled by Jesus. (Scholars have actually identified 322 distinct prophecies.) God has declared that prophecy is the key test to determine whether something is "from Him" (Deuteronomy 18:9-22; Isaiah 46:10). Certainly the Jews themselves were well aware of a coming Messiah ("anointed one"). Perhaps the single most important indication of the coming Messiah in relation to the Trinity is Isaiah's prophecy of a "son" who was to be called "Immanuel" (Isaiah 7:14).

Immanuel means:
"God with us"

Matthew makes this prophetic parallel very clear in his Gospel (Matthew 1:23).

> ## Melchizedek—Christ in the Old Testament?
>
> Some scholars believe that Christ appeared in the Old Testament era. Melchizedek—whom Abram (later Abraham) encountered—may be such a case. At least he is a "model" of Jesus (Genesis 14:18).
>
> Melchizedek was honored as a "priest of God Most High" (Hebrews 7:1,2)—just as Jesus is a priest. He offered Abram bread and wine, possibly a foreshadowing of the last supper. And Abram gave him a tenth of everything, an early example of the tithe which was later instituted in the Law of Moses.

The early Apostles, who lived continuously with Jesus for three years, not only understood the important role of the Son, Jesus, as part of the Trinity—they actually used the Old Testament prophecy of a coming "God incarnate" to persuade the monotheistic* Jews that Jesus was God. When we consider the very strong

---

* "Monotheistic" means "believing in a single God." "Monotheism" means "belief in a single God."

monotheistic attitude of the Jewish nation, and add to this the very large number of Jews who quickly adopted Christianity (largely due to fulfilled Old Testament prophecy), this leads us to the conclusion that those who were in the best position to "know for certain" the facts about Jesus (including His role as a person of the Trinity) accepted the prophecy about Jesus, including Matthew's key point of Jesus being "God with us."

God the Spirit

The third component of the Trinity, the Spirit of God, is mentioned throughout the Old Testament. Starting at the very beginning of Genesis (1:2), we find this important verse:

> "...and the Spirit of God was hovering over
> the surface of the waters."

The Hebrew word used for spirit is *ruwach*, which in essence means "a resemblance of breath"—but "only by a rational being."[10] So we can recognize immediately that this "Spirit" is differentiated from God the Father and God the Son. And we also see that He is a "rational being," not merely some "force." Furthermore, we see the Holy Spirit being involved immediately from the beginning of creation.

The Spirit of God is also seen in the Old Testament as a counselor or helper—indwelling people to allow them to accomplish things that God wills (as in the New Testament). For example, Bezalel was filled with the Spirit of God so that he would have certain abilities in handcrafts to use in making the tabernacle (Exodus 31:3). Even some people who *rejected* God were inspired by the Holy Spirit, as indicated by the pagan prophet Balaam's blessing of Israel despite the enemy king Balak's attempt to purchase a curse (Numbers 24:2,3).

The Trinity in the New Testament

The concept of the Trinity is clearly expressed throughout the New Testament. If we accept the Bible as truth (see pages 6–9), we do not need to wonder about the doctrine of the Trinity, because we have distinct evidence from both the start of Jesus' ministry and also the end, with a great deal of supporting evidence in between.

The Beginning of Jesus' Ministry

When Jesus was about 30 years old, He started His ministry by being baptized by John the Baptist. It's significant to note that Jesus appeared very human and humble. John said of Jesus, "He will baptize you with the Holy Spirit and with fire" (Matthew 3:11).

Notice the inclusion of all three persons of the Trinity in this verse: Jesus, the "Holy Spirit," and "fire" (which was a manifestation of God in the Old Testament—see Exodus 3:2; 13:21). John claimed to be "unworthy" of baptizing Jesus; then, when the baptism took place (at Jesus' insistence), we again find all three persons of the Trinity:

The Son: was humbly submitting Himself in human form to the Father, as a model for all the world (Matthew 3).

The Father: spoke from heaven saying "This is my Son, whom I love; with him I am well pleased" (Matthew 3:17).

The Holy Spirit: The "Spirit of God" descended "like a dove," lighting on Jesus (Matthew 3:16).

The End of Jesus' Ministry

The last words of a person are often the most significant. After all, we all want to leave the people we love with the most important thing we want them to remember. (Advertising is an ideal example. The last words are almost always the brand name and the primary attribute—often a slogan). Keeping this in mind, what were the last words of Jesus?

We can find those words spoken just prior to His ascension into heaven, in Matthew 28:19,20. He said,

> "Therefore go and make disciples of all nations, baptizing them in the name of the *Father* and of the *Son* and of the *Holy Spirit*, and teaching them to obey everything I have commanded you. And surely I am with you always, to the very end of the age."

No doubt Jesus especially wanted people to recognize the three-in-one nature of God. Otherwise, why would He use His final words to emphasize the three persons of the Trinity?

Baptism is an important part of one's commitment to the Christian faith and to Jesus Christ. So Jesus' last commandment (often called the "Great Commission") deals with the issue of a public proclamation—baptism—during which all three persons of the Godhead are recognized—the Father, the Son, and the Holy Spirit. Hence, when people are baptized as Christians, the Trinity is an integral part of their commitment.

More New Testament References

The New Testament differentiates, yet also unites, the Father, the Son, and the Holy Spirit in many ways (in addition to those indicated at the beginning and end of Jesus' ministry). For example, Paul speaks of God's three-in-one nature in his letter to Corinth. He describes the differences in roles, but the oneness of "essence":

> "There are *different kinds of gifts*, but the *same Spirit*. There are *different kinds of service*, but the *same Lord*. There are *different kinds of working*, but the *same God* works all of them in all men."
> —*1 Corinthians 12:4-6*

And the clear distinction in the roles of the three persons of the Trinity was laid out by Jesus, who spoke of His role as intercessor, the Father's as the ultimate authority, and the Holy Spirit's as our helper in day-to-day decisions in the following verse:

> "*I* will ask the *Father*, and he will give you
> another *Counselor* to be with you forever—the *Spirit* of truth.
> The world cannot accept him,
> because it neither sees him nor knows him."
> —*Jesus, in John 14:16,17*

God's Love in the Trinity

God existed as the Trinity before time began (Genesis 1:1; 1:26; John 1). Yet the reality of God's love has been displayed in His three-in-one nature since before anything else existed. God's total and complete love is shown forth in the three persons as they exemplify grace, love, and fellowship:

> "May the *grace of the Lord Jesus Christ*,
> and the *love of God*, and the *fellowship of the Holy Spirit* be with you all."
> —*2 Corinthians 13:14*

Grace: The Son—Jesus' death provided the grace we need.

Love: The Father—His love was fully defined through Jesus' sacrifice.

Some References to the Triune God in the New Testament

- Matthew 3:16,17
- John 14:16
- 1 Corinthians 12:4-6
- 2 Corinthians 13:14
- Ephesians 3:14-19
- Ephesians 4:4-13
- 1 Peter 1:1,2
- Revelation 1:4-6

Fellowship: The Holy Spirit—He continually strengthens and guides us.

We see an indication of both the co-equality of the Holy Trinity and the love of the Trinity expressed in John 3:16:

> "God so loved the world, that he gave his one and only Son, that whoever believes in him shall not perish but have eternal life."

The Son, Jesus, is sent to reconcile humans with God—"Grace and truth came through Jesus Christ" (John 1:17). The sending of Jesus in the very first place was because of God the Father's love for human beings. And the Holy Spirit unites human beings in fellowship with God.

One God in Three Persons

GOD is...

The SON (Jesus)
- The **Redeemer**
- The **Source of life** for humans
- An **Intercessor** with the Father

GOD is...

...Meets All Human Needs

The FATHER
- The **Authority**
- **Perfect** in holiness
- The **Receiver** of worship in heaven

GOD is...

COMPLETE
- An **Authority** to worship
- A **Redeemer** for forgiveness
- A **Counselor** to guide

The HOLY SPIRIT
- The **Counselor**
- A **Comforter** in hardship
- An **Agent** of the Father's will

The Persons of the Trinity Described

The Father—The First Person of the Godhead

A precise description of the person of the Father is beyond human ability and comprehension. Though it was believed that anyone who "saw the face of God would die" (Genesis 32:30; Isaiah 6:1-5), the glory of God was displayed in the Old Testament to the Israelites several times (see pages 14–17). It was also expressed audibly at the baptism of Jesus (Matthew 3:17) and at the transfiguration (Matthew 17:5).

John's revelation from Jesus provides some clues as to the appearance of the Father. He describes Him as "someone" sitting on a throne in heaven. He has the "appearance of jasper and carnelian," and from His throne come "flashes of lightning" and "peals of thunder" (Revelation 4:3,5)—similar to the glory of God at Mt. Sinai (Exodus 19:16-18). Finally, God is often referred to as "light" (for example, in 1 John 1:5). Whether this is a reference to the Father alone or the entire Godhead is not clear. However, God Himself is called a light so incredible as to eliminate the need for the sun or for lamps (Revelation 22:5).

It is important to point out that the Bible's teaching stresses the essence of God the Father, not as being a physical human father, but as being a heavenly Father—the Creator of all things (Job 38:4-7; Psalm 33:6).

The Son—The Second Person of the Godhead

Jesus, the Son, was fully human and fully God (John 10:30). Therefore, the physical being of Jesus is completely that of a human. Jesus was conceived through the Holy Spirit within a human body—the body of Mary (Luke 1:35; Matthew 1:20). However, to Jesus' complete human nature was joined the complete nature of God, and both natures were in one person, Jesus. This made it easy for us to relate to God, and for Jesus to experience everything we experience (Hebrews 2:9,12,18). It also provided the necessary utterly perfect sacrifice for sin (Hebrews 10:1-14).

Perhaps the most difficult thing about Jesus to understand from our limited human viewpoint is Jesus' preexistence. We know that Jesus was co-eternal with God, since He was there in the beginning and then came to earth.

"In the beginning was the Word."
—John 1:1

"The Word became flesh and made
his dwelling among us."
—John 1:14

Jesus as the Son never referred to His special relationship with the Father in a way that might imply that the disciples had an equal relationship. Jesus claimed to be the preexistent eternal Son, fully God and fully equal with the Father, incarnated to fulfill God's purpose of providing salvation. For this reason He was appointed as the sole mediator between humans and God the Father (Matthew 11:27; John 5:22; 8:58; 10:30,38; 14:9; 16:28). As a human who was also fully God, Jesus accepted prayer and worship (Matthew 14:33; 28:9; John 14:14).

The Holy Spirit—The Third Person of the Godhead

The original Hebrew and Greek words referring to the Holy Spirit (*ruwach* and *pneuma*) mean "wind" or "breath." We cannot see wind, but we know it exists. The Holy Spirit is the all-powerful and personal force of God that was involved in Creation (Genesis 1:2) and will be involved at the end of time summoning people into the new heaven and earth (Revelation 22:17). The Holy Spirit is involved with human beings who are believers on a daily basis as a "comforter," guiding us, communicating the presence of the living Christ to us, and doing everything for us that Christ Himself did for the disciples (John 14:15-17; 16:13-15). He is an invisible supporter of good (Zechariah 4:6; 1 Corinthians 12:3) and restrainer and convicter of evil (Genesis 6:3; John 16:8-11; 1 Corinthians 12:3).

The Three-in-One Nature of the Trinity

Could We Ever Understand a Multidimensional God?

Though the concept of the Trinity has been known since the time of Christ, it has often been misunderstood. Why? Because humans exist in a world that consists of three dimensions of space and one dimension of time. How can we know or even, sometimes, conceive of dimensions beyond our own—such as the spiritual dimension? This has been a large problem for people who can't accept God because He is too far beyond our understanding.

The Bible is very clear in its references to the triune nature of God (see pages 14–23). We also know there was a widespread, rapid acceptance of Jesus as God (co-equal with the Father) by the Jews around Jerusalem in the months immediately after Jesus' death. At first glance, this would seem to contradict the traditional Jewish monotheism (was Jesus an "additional" god?). Yet the early Jewish Christians accepted Jesus as "one" with the Father: co-existent and co-equal.

God Is Light

There are many analogies to the Trinity in the physical world: An egg consists of three equally important parts—the shell, the white, and the yolk—yet all are one; time is one, yet it consists of the past, present, and future; and one colleague of mine even stated that Neapolitan ice cream is one, yet consists of chocolate, vanilla, and strawberry. No analogy can adequately comprehend an infinite God. Perhaps the best one, though, is God's own description of Himself: "God is light" (1 John 1:5).

Physicists know that light is comprised of three distinct yet indivisibly interrelated properties: wave, material (photons), and quantum. Though each property reveals itself in a different way, they are nonetheless each all "light." Likewise, light is comprised of electro-magnetic waves of different frequencies. At the low end of the spectrum, we have radio waves—which, given the proper transforming device, can be heard. In the middle, we have visible waves—which can be seen. At the upper end, we have infrared waves—which can be felt as heat. Perhaps light is a model of the Trinity?

God Created Man in His Own Image

The record of the beginning describes humans as being created in God's image (Genesis 1:27). Does that mean we look like God? No. It means that our basic essence is like the essence of God (yet we are not God). We have a physical essence, which parallels Jesus, God the Son. We have a spiritual essence, which parallels the Holy Spirit. And we have a yearning to be in union with a father* (God the Father). Hence, the Trinity is similar to the basic components of God's image in human beings.

The Expression of God's Love Required the Full Resources of the Trinity

In order to demonstrate complete love to human beings, who were made in the image of God, all three persons of God are necessary. First, an authority figure (the Father) was necessary to display perfect love, justice, and holiness. The Father provided us a chance to love Him perfectly by giving us free choice—which also allowed sin to enter the world. Second, a human figure (the Son, Jesus) was necessary 1) to give Himself as the perfect sacrifice to redeem humans from the sin He knew they would choose, and 2) to be our ongoing source of life and relationship with the Father. Finally, the Holy Spirit was necessary to provide humans daily guidance, assurance, and counsel by being the continual presence of Christ within us.

* In fact, it is God the Father from whom the very concept of fatherhood originates, as Paul seems to indicate in Ephesians 3:14,15: "...I kneel before the Father, from whom his whole family in heaven and on earth devices its name."

The Roles of the Trinity in God's Creation and Plan

God's Creation

All three persons of the Trinity were present at the creation of the world. The creation was accomplished by God (Hebrew *Elohiym*) acting as Father, Son, and Holy Spirit. As already noted, *Elohiym* represents a plural yet single God (see page 14). Specifically, the creation event involves each member of the Trinity in the following ways:

Father: The direction came from His ultimate authority. This is explicitly declared in Revelation, when the Father is honored on His throne as Creator:

> "You are worthy, our Lord and God, to receive glory
> and honor and power, for you created all things,
> and by your will they were created and have their being."
> —*Revelation 4:11*

Son: The Word of God. Present from the beginning, it was He through whom God "made the universe" (Hebrews 1:1,2). This is reiterated in John's Gospel:

> "In the beginning was the Word,
> and the Word was with God, and the Word was God.
> He was with God in the beginning.
> Through him all things were made;
> without him nothing was made that has been made.
> ...And the Word became flesh and made his dwelling among us."
> —*John 1:1,14*

Holy Spirit: The empowerment of God. The frame of reference for the creation of the earth was not a faraway impersonal god or force, but the Spirit of God who hovered over the surface of the waters (Genesis 1:2—see page 17). The Spirit's role is further described by the manner in which God works through Him ("breath" and "wind" are references to the Spirit):

"By the word of the LORD were the heavens made, their
starry host by the breath of his mouth."
—*Psalm 33:6*

God's Plan

God's overall plan for human beings can be defined by examining the roles of each of the persons of the Trinity.

Father: The will of the plan of God. Revealed at the creation of the world (see Revelation 4:11 on previous page), it is also defined in Paul's letter to the Ephesians:

"In him we were also chosen, having been predestined
according to the *plan of him who works out everything
in conformity with the purpose of his will,*
in order that we, who were the first to hope in Christ,
might be for the praise of his glory."
—*Ephesians 1:11,12*

Son: The execution of the plan of God. Jesus was the literal sacrifice that redeemed human beings to God and reconciled them with God, as He knew and had planned since the beginning of time.

"...Yet for us there is but one God, the Father,
from whom all things came and for whom we live;
and there is but one Lord, Jesus Christ,
through whom all things came and *through whom we live.*"
—*1 Corinthians 8:6*

Jesus' role in the plan of God is further explained in Paul's letter to the Colossians:

"He is the *image of the invisible God,*
the firstborn over all creation.
For by him all things were created:
things in heaven and on earth, visible and invisible,
whether thrones or powers or rulers or authorities;
all things were *created by him and for him.*"
—*Colossians 1:15,16*

Holy Spirit: The wisdom of God. The Holy Spirit provides wisdom in the direction of God's plan through individuals chosen by God.

> "The Spirit of the LORD will rest on him—
> the *Spirit of wisdom*
> and of understanding,
> the *Spirit of counsel and of power*,
> the *Spirit of knowledge* and of the fear of the LORD—
> and he will delight in the fear of the LORD."
> —*Isaiah 11:2,3*

> "'Not by might nor by power, *but by my Spirit*,'
> says the LORD Almighty."
> —*Zechariah 4:6*

The Provision of God's Word

The Word of God as revealed in the Bible is the incredible masterpiece that God uses to reveal His love to human beings and to guide us in our daily life here on earth. All three persons of the Holy Trinity were involved in the giving of the Word.

Father: The revelation of the Word of God:

> "So is my *word* that goes out from my mouth:
> It will not return to me empty."
> —*Isaiah 55:11*

Son: The realized Word of God:

> "The *Word became flesh* and made
> his dwelling among us."
> —*John 1:14*

> "The Son is the radiance of God's glory
> and the exact representation of his being,
> sustaining all things by his powerful word."
> —*Hebrews 1:3*

Holy Spirit: The expressed Word of God. Often when we don't know what to say, or how to react, the Spirit of God does it for us:

"We have not received the spirit of the world but the Spirit
who is from God, that we may understand
what God has freely given us.
This is what we speak, not in words taught us
by human wisdom but in words taught by the Spirit,
expressing spiritual truths in spiritual words.
The man without the Spirit does not accept the things
that come from the Spirit of God, for they are foolishness
to him, and he cannot understand them."
—*1 Corinthians 2:12-14*

The Roles of the Trinity in Reuniting People with God

People are separated from God. Bible-based Christians relate this to the original sin by Adam and Eve in the garden of Eden (Genesis 3). But even if this seems to some people like an unrealistic event, virtually everyone feels cut off from God in some way, regardless of who he or she thinks God is.

The Trinity is an essential ingredient to restoring that relationship because it fully takes into account our *humanity* (through the Son, Jesus), our *spirit* (through the Holy Spirit), and our need to rely upon and commune with an *authority* (through the Father). The Triune God provides the perfect, complete means to reconcile us with Himself—1) the sacrifice of Jesus and 2) the ongoing prompting of the Holy Spirit to bring us back into fellowship with 3) the "Father figure"—the entire omnipotent, omnipresent Godhead.

God's Advent in Human Form as Jesus

A sacrifice on a "creature" level was necessary to purge human beings of sin. This is indicated in Leviticus and Deuteronomy and throughout the rest of the Torah (the first five books of the Bible, which were written by Moses). But only a perfect sacrifice of a perfect human being would suffice for the purging of mankind. By implication, only God Himself could be such a sacrifice. And He was—in the human form of Jesus. The Scripture shows all three persons of the Trinity working in this:

Father: The directing of God's advent. Jesus submitted to the direction of the Father. He recognized His role as a perfect human sacrifice to take away the sin of all who accepted him. Jesus' body replaced the inadequate and temporary animal offerings that were commanded in the Law of Moses.

"Therefore, when Christ came into the world, he said:
'Sacrifice and offering you did not desire,
but a body you prepared for me;
with burnt offerings and sin offerings
you were not pleased.
Then I said, "Here I am—it is written about me
in the scroll—I have come to do your will, O God."'"
—*Hebrews 10:5-7*

Son: The expression of God's advent. The entire Gospel of Matthew discusses Jesus as the Messiah who was also the Son of God. Matthew's book records several instances where Jesus was confirmed as the Son of God.

"'But what about you?' He asked. 'Who do you say I am?'
Simon Peter answered, 'You are the Christ, the Son of the living
God.' Jesus replied, 'Blessed are you, Simon son of Jonah,
for this was not revealed to you by man,
but by my Father in heaven.'"
—*Matthew 16:15-17*

Holy Spirit: The empowerment of God's advent. The Holy Spirit was sent to enable the conception of Jesus as a human being.

"Joseph son of David, do not be afraid to take Mary home as
your wife, because what is conceived in her is
from the Holy Spirit."
—*Matthew 1:20*

"The one whom God has sent speaks the words of God,
for God gives the Spirit without limit."
—*John 3:34*

Salvation Through Jesus' Sacrifice

God's enormous triumph over sin was accomplished with all three persons of the Trinity intimately involved:

Father: The sending of the Son was from the Father:

> "God so loved the world that he gave his one
> and only Son, that whoever believes in him
> shall not perish but have eternal life."
> —John 3:16

> "This is love: not that we loved God, but that he loved us
> and sent his Son as an atoning sacrifice for our sins."
> —1 John 4:10,11

Son: The sacrifice was carried out by Jesus. The word translated for "finished" in the Scripture below also means "paid in full," as with a debt—or as a ransom of human beings from sin:

> "Jesus said, 'It is finished.' With that, he bowed
> his head and gave up his spirit."
> —John 19:30

> "Christ was sacrificed once to take away
> the sins of many people."
> —Hebrews 9:28

Holy Spirit: The Holy Spirit provided support of the mission of Jesus by filling Him with the presence of the living God:

> "The one whom God has sent speaks the words
> of God, for God gives the Spirit without limit."
> —John 3:34

Reconciliation with God

Jesus' sacrifice enabled people to be reconciled with God by simply accepting it for themselves, thereby making Jesus Lord and Savior. Again, all three persons of the Trinity had a role:

Father: Fellowship was restored with the Father:

> "We proclaim to you what we have seen and heard, so that
> you also may have fellowship with us. And our fellowship is
> with the Father and with his Son, Jesus Christ."
> —1 John 1:3

Son: Jesus became the *Liberator* of human beings—freeing them from Satan through His death on the cross so they could be reconciled with God:

"[Jesus] says, 'Here am I, and the children God has given me.' Since the children have flesh and blood, he too shared in their humanity so that by his death he might destroy him who holds the power of death—that is, the devil—and free those who all their lives were held in slavery by their fear of death."
—*Hebrews 2:13-15*

Holy Spirit: The Holy Spirit is the means of renewed fellowship between God and human beings. This is apparent in the salutation of Paul's second letter to the church in Corinth in which he emphasizes the three roles of the persons of the Godhead, stressing the fellowship as the role of the Holy Spirit:

"May the grace of the Lord Jesus Christ, and the love of God, and the fellowship of the Holy Spirit be with you all."
—*2 Corinthians 13:14*

The Roles of the Trinity in Developing Virtues and Holiness

Once people are brought into a new relationship with God by accepting the God-given sacrifice of Jesus, the rest of their life on earth is a period of development. God "goes to work" inside believers, helping them display the holiness and virtue that He has granted them in Christ. (This is regardless of where they were in the past, because each person who "is in Christ...is a new creation; the old has gone, the new has come!"—see 2 Corinthians 5:17.)

"Sanctification" is the word commonly used to describe this process.* All three persons of the Trinity have roles in this lifelong event, but it's of special importance to recognize the role of Jesus, the Son. Why? Because He is the One who displays the imperceptible multidimensional God in visible human form.

As God the Son, Jesus is both the revealer of God the Father and the Source of Life to human beings.

> "No one has ever seen God, but God the Only Begotten [the Son], who is at the Father's side, has made him known."
> —John 1:18

> "All things have been committed to me by my Father. No one knows the Son except the Father, and no one knows the Father except the Son and those to whom the Son chooses to reveal him."
> —Jesus, in Matthew 11:27

> "In him was life, and that life was the light of men."
> —John 1:4

> "I am the way and the truth and the *life*."
> —Jesus, in John 14:6

As the "Son of Man" (the name Jesus most often used of Himself), Jesus is the perfect human being. Why? Because through the Holy Spirit, He lived a life that was completely dependent upon the

---

* "Sanctification" is being set apart for or dedicated to a special purpose, especially God's purpose.

Father. Jesus gives this kind of life to those who believe in Him, and they in turn live in Him. A Christian's daily life is "in Him."

> "He [Jesus] was even calling God his own Father, making himself equal with God. Jesus gave them this answer, 'I tell you the truth, the Son can do nothing by himself. He can only do what he sees his Father doing, because whatever the Father does the Son also does.'"
> —John 5:18,19

> "Because I live, you also will live. On that day [the day of the Spirit's coming, which happened a few weeks later], you will realize that I am in my Father, and *you are in me, and I am in you.*"
> —Jesus, in John 14:19-20

The Provision of Holiness to Believers

Because God came to earth in the form of Jesus and has "taken up residence" inside believers, we can love with His kind of love, and have faith and hope. All three persons of the Trinity play a role in giving holiness to us.

Father: The *standard* of holiness:

> "Just as he who called you is holy, so be holy in all you do; for it is written: 'Be holy, because I am holy.'"
> —1 Peter 1:15,16

Son: The *Source* of holiness:

> "You are in Christ Jesus, who has become for us wisdom from God—that is, our righteousness, holiness and redemption."
> —1 Corinthians 1:30

Holy Spirit: The *daily provider* of holiness:

> "So I say, live by the Spirit, and you will not gratify the desires of the flesh."
> —Galatians 5:16

"What the law was powerless to do in that it was weakened by
the flesh, God did by sending his own Son in the likeness of
sinful man to be a sin offering. And so he condemned sin in the
flesh, in order that the righteous requirements of the law might
be fully met in us, who do not live according to the flesh
but according to the Spirit."
—*Romans 8:3,4*

The Provision of Love, Faith, and Hope

The Trinity is involved in the giving of love, faith, and hope.
These three things are often spoken of together in the New
Testament.

Father: The love of the Father is apparent, and is essentially the
basis for all Christianity, through His gift of Jesus:

"God so loved the world that he gave his one
and only Son, that whoever believes in him shall not
perish but have eternal life."
—*John 3:16*

Son: Jesus is the object of faith and indicated that He is the
one way to know God by faith. For the believer, He is the Source
of faith:

"I am the way and the truth and the life. No one
comes to the Father except through me."
—*Jesus, in John 14:6*

"Let us fix our eyes on Jesus, the author and perfecter of our
faith, who for the joy set before him endured the cross,
scorning its shame, and sat down at the right hand of the
throne of God."
—*Hebrews 12:2,3*

Holy Spirit: The Holy Spirit provides hope to all who know Jesus:

"May the God of hope fill you with all joy and peace
as you trust in him, so that you may overflow
with hope by the power of the Holy Spirit."
—*Romans 15:13*

The Provision of Spiritual Gifts

God has generously provided spiritual gifts to each of us to help
us in our new life in Christ as we work for the good of other
people. This provision involves the Trinity in using humanity to
help humanity (see Mark 12:31—God's second-greatest commandment; also 4:3-13):

"He [the Spirit] will bring glory to me by taking from what is
mine and making it known to you. All that belongs to the
Father is mine. That is why I said the Spirit will take from what
is mine and make it known to you."
—*Jesus, in John 16:14,15*

"To each one the manifestation of the Spirit is
given for the common good."
—*1 Corinthians 12:7*

Some of the gifts of the Spirit:

1. Wisdom
2. Knowledge
3. Faith
4. Healing
5. Miracles
6. Prophecy
7. Discernment (distinguishing between spirits)
8. Speaking in "tongues" (that is, languages other
    than one's own)
9. Interpretation of tongues

"All these are the work of one and the same Spirit, and
he gives them to each one, just as he determines."
—*1 Corinthians 12:11*

The Trinity Is Necessary for Eternal Life with God

We have looked at the roles of each person of the Trinity—and the biblical support for them—from Creation, through the reconciliation of humans with God, to the development of virtues and holiness in a believer's life (see pages 28–39). We can see that:

1. The concept of the Trinity is clear throughout the Bible, and

2. Each person of the Trinity had a clear role from the beginning in all human relationships with God.

Yet we are still left with the question,

> "Why was a Triune God necessary in the first place?"

Just asking that question (though many people have) seems somewhat ridiculous. How can we ask God why He is what He is? Even so, though it is impossible for human minds to comprehend an infinite God, the Bible does give us some clues why the Trinity is necessary for our eternal relationship with God. Consider these points.

1. God is perfectly holy. He was once in complete fellowship with a sinless Adam and Eve.

2. Once Adam and Eve sinned, humanity became separated from God.

3. A perfect blood sacrifice was required to pay for human sin.

4. Even after the giving of this perfect sacrifice, humans still continue to sin.

5. God's ultimate goal is complete fellowship with humans in a perfectly sinless place (heaven).

God—The Father

The Father loves human beings—but their sin set them apart from Him, to the point that anyone seeing His face would die. He is the essence of holiness. Eventually it is He to whom all people will bow down in worship. But the remedy for His separation from the humans He loved required a sacrifice—the sacrifice of Himself.

Jesus—The Son

The only sacrifice "good enough" for a perfectly holy God, adequate to buy back humans from sin, was the sacrifice of God Himself—His Son Jesus. This required God to come to earth in human form, His ultimate mission being the giving of this sacrifice, revealing to human beings everything that God wanted us to know about Himself.

The Holy Spirit

Since those members of the human race who received Jesus would continue to face problems and struggles with sin in their new life in Christ, Jesus sent a "Counselor" and Helper to live inside them, someone who could touch their minds and hearts. All this would be for the goal of "character development" (sanctification), readying people to be with God in heaven forever.

Why Some People Reject the Trinity

The Trinity Is a Difficult Concept

How could we possibly understand something that is beyond all our senses, which are our means of input? We can't. We need to expand our thinking to dimensions beyond those in which we live and trust the guidance we get from the Bible (which has already shown that it was influenced by a God beyond our space-time domain—see pages 6–9).

There are many things we humans find difficult to understand. Take for example the fact that water (H_2O) can exist as a gas (steam), a liquid (water), and a solid (ice) if held at the proper temperatures and pressures. Only engineers and physicists understand why. Or consider light, which has particle, wave, and quantum properties. Again, it's difficult to understand, but it's true.

The same thing could be said of the Trinity. It's difficult to understand because it's outside of our human experience, but it's still clear from the biblical account—and it is true. But unfortunately, many people are quick to accept "scientific evidence" while rejecting the Bible's teaching.

Some Religions That Reject the Trinity

Hinduism—The Hindu religion rejects Jesus, and therefore rejects the Trinity.

Buddhism—Since most Buddhists reject a personal God, they also reject the Trinity.

Shintoism—This philosophy doesn't deal with the issues of the Trinity.

Confucianism and Taoism—These philosophies don't deal with the issues of the Trinity.

Islam—Jesus is considered a great prophet, but not God, hence Muslims don't accept the Trinity.

Judaism—Followers of Judaism consider Jesus a real person, but not God, thus they don't accept the Trinity.

Jehovah's Witnesses—They consider Jesus real, but not God, hence they reject the Trinity.

Mormons—Jesus is considered a god alongside many others.

Christian Scientists—Jesus is considered to be god *in part*, just like everyone else.

Unity Church of Christianity—Jesus is considered to be god *in part*, just like everyone else.

The Way International—Members of "The Way" consider Jesus a man, not God; hence they don't accept the Trinity.

New Age (many versions)—New Age concepts of Jesus vary, but essentially God is everything, and the Trinity doesn't matter (much like Hinduism).

Scientology—Jesus is not an issue.

The Unification Church ("Moonies")—Jesus is viewed as real, but not as God, thus the Unification Church doesn't accept the Trinity.

Common Questions

Wouldn't a Loving God Allow Good People into Heaven?

Many people believe that living a good life and being kind to others is the way to heaven. Naturally, they are thinking of a "good" life in terms of our distorted human view; and such a life is far from God's standard. The Bible says that the *only* way to God the Father in heaven is through Jesus Christ (John 14:6). So will loving and "good" people who don't accept Jesus go to hell? Yes—but how can they be truly good if they reject the love of God's Son, Jesus, who died for them?

God will allow perfectly good people into heaven. But His standard of goodness is the perfection of His Son Jesus. Hence, there is simply no other way to come to Him except through Jesus— let alone the fact that every sin of mind or body we commit removes us further from Jesus' perfection (Matthew 5:28,29; Romans 3:22,23).

Everyone is imperfect, but the good news is that God has provided Jesus as a perfect sacrifice for us. He is our way to heaven. Not accepting God's gift of love and forgiveness through Jesus, despite the Holy Spirit's prompting, is unforgivable (Mark 3:29).

How Can We Ensure the Right Relationship So We Can Go to Heaven?

When Jesus said that not all who use His name will enter heaven (Matthew 7:21-23), He was referring to people who think using Christ's name along with rules and rituals is the key to heaven. A *relationship* with God is not based on rituals or rules. It's based on grace, forgiveness, and the right standing with Him through Jesus Christ.

How to Have a Personal Relationship with God

1. *Believe that God exists* and that He came to earth in the human form of Jesus Christ (John 3:16; Romans 10:9).

2. *Accept God's free forgiveness of sins and gift of new life* through the death and resurrection of Jesus Christ (Ephesians 2:8-10; 1:7,8).

3. *Switch to God's plan for your life* (1 Peter 1:21-23; Ephesians 2:1-7).

4. *Expressly make Jesus Christ the Director* of your life (Matthew 7:21-27; 1 John 4:15).

Prayer for Eternal Life with God

"Dear God, I believe You sent Your Son, Jesus, to die for my sins so I can be forgiven. I'm sorry for my sins, and I want to live the rest of my life the way You want me to. Please put Your Spirit in my life to direct me. Amen."

Then What?

People who sincerely take these steps become members of God's family of believers. A new world of freedom and strength is available through Jesus' life within you, expressing itself through prayer and obedience to God's will. The new relationship can be strengthened by taking the following steps:

- Find a Bible-based church that you like and attend regularly.
- Set aside some time each day to pray and read the Bible.
- Locate other Christians to spend time with on a regular basis.

God's Promises to Believers

For Today

"Seek first his kingdom and his righteousness, and all these things [things to satisfy all your needs] will be given to you as well."
—*Matthew 6:33*

For Eternity

"Whoever believes in the Son has eternal life, but whoever rejects the Son will not see life, for God's wrath remains on him."
—*John 3:36*

Once we develop an eternal perspective, even the greatest problems on earth fade in significance.

Notes

Note: The author does not agree with *all* authors below on *all* viewpoints. Each reference has some findings worthy of consideration. (*"Test everything"* —1 Thessalonians 5:21).

1. Muncaster, Ralph O., *Does the Bible Predict the Future?*, Eugene, OR: Harvest House, 2000.

2. Muncaster, Ralph O., *Science—Was the Bible Ahead of Its Time?*, Eugene, OR: Harvest House, 2000.

3. Muncaster, Ralph O., *Can You Trust the Bible?*, Eugene, OR: Harvest House, 2000.

4. Muncaster, Ralph O., *Can Archaeology Prove the New Testament?*, Eugene, OR: Harvest House, 2000.

5. McDowell, Josh, and Wilson, Bill, *A Ready Defense*, San Bernardino, CA: Here's Life Publishers, Inc., 1990.

6. Muncaster, Ralph O., *How Do We Know Jesus Is God?*, Eugene, OR: Harvest House, 2000.

7. Muncaster, Ralph O., *What Is the Proof for the Resurrection?*, Eugene, OR: Harvest House, 2000.

8. *Webster's II New Riverside University Dictionary*, Riverside, CA: The Riverside Publishing Company, 1976.

9. Elwell, Walter A. (Editor), *Evangelical Dictionary of Theology*, Grand Rapids, MI: Baker Book House Co., 1984.

10. Zodhiates, Spiros, *The Complete Word Study of the Old Testament*, Chattanooga, TN: AMG Publishers, 1994.

Bibliography

Ankerberg, John, and Weldon, John, *Knowing the Truth About the Trinity*, Eugene, OR: Harvest House Publishers, 1997.

Bickersteth, Edward Henry, *The Trinity: The Classical Study of Biblical Trinitarianism*, Grand Rapids, MI: Kregel Publishing,

Geisler, Norman, PhD, and Brooks, Ron, *When Skeptics Ask*, Grand Rapids, MI: Baker Books, 1990.

Life Application Bible, Wheaton, IL: Tyndale House Publishers, and Grand Rapids, MI: Zondervan Publishing House, 1991.

McDowell, Josh, *Handbook of Today's Religions*, San Bernardino, CA: Campus Crusade for Christ, 1983.

Swindoll, Charles R., *The Trinity: Discovering the Depth of the Nature of God*, Nashville, TN: Broadman & Holman, 1986.

Smith, F. LaGard, *The Daily Bible in Chronological Order*, Eugene, OR: Harvest House, 1984.

Walvoord, John F., *The Prophecy Knowledge Handbook*, Wheaton, IL: Victor Books, 1990.

White, James R., *The Forgotten Trinity: Recovering the Heart of Christian Belief*, Minneapolis, MN: Bethany House Publishers, 1998.

Youngblood, Ronald F., *New Illustrated Bible Dictionary*, Nashville, TN: Thomas Nelson, 1995.

Zodhiates, Spiros, *The Complete Word Study of the New Testament*, Chattanooga, TN: AMG Publishers, 1991.